Peter Eldin

The Whizzkid's Handbook 3

with drawings by Roger Smith

An Armada Original

The Whizzkid's Handbook 3 was first published in
Armada in 1983 by Fontana Paperbacks,
8 Grafton Street, London W1X 3LA.

© Eldin Editorial Services 1983

Printed in Great Britain by
William Collins Sons & Co., Ltd., Glasgow

Wrigglesworth (well-known bookworm)

Contents

Foreword

There used to be a time when the only thing you needed to find your way through school was a map. Nowadays things are a little more complicated and you require an expert sherpa guide. That is what this book and the two previous *Whizzkid's Handbooks* are designed to be – expert guides (or boy scouts) for schoolkids, to help them on their painful and precarious way through school.

As a result of the success of the first two books I have visited many schools in the British Isles. Luckily I have always managed to escape again. During my visits, many Whizzkids have passed on suggestions for this book – "Why don't you burn it?", "Use it to prop up a rickety piano", or "Make paper aeroplanes with the pages" are typical of the ones polite enough to be repeated. Some of your ideas that were not too outrageous have been smuggled past the censor and appear here for the benefit of all.

I hope that you enjoy this new book.

Whizzkid's rule, OK?

Peter Eldin

Card for the Teacher

When it is your teacher's birthday buy him or her a birthday card (bet you didn't even know teachers *were* actually born!). If you cannot afford a card you can easily make one of your own.

Put glue on the inner surfaces of the card but leave the edges unstuck. Now close the card so the two pages stick together. Because the edges are not glued the card appears quite ordinary.

Write on the front of the card: "Only bright and intelligent people can open this card." Get someone else to give the card to the teacher – preferably on a day you are away from school!

How to Upset a Dinner Lady

If you go to school dinners regularly you are very brave. It may be that you are brave enough to make some funny, but not too rude, comments to the dinner lady without upsetting her too much. She may even come to the conclusion that you are a wit – a nit wit.

Irish stew	Ah, the policeman's favourite meal –Irish stew in the name of the law.
Dumplings	Can I take one home? I need a new cricket ball.
Curry	Can I take this home in a curryer bag?
Steak	I've heard of being burned at the steak, but this steak is really burned.
Fish	It looks as if it has had its chips.
Fishfingers	What have you done with the thumbs?
Shepherd's pie	Is it made with real shepherds?
Treacle tart	Can I take a barrow load? My dad wants to lay a garden path.
Cottage pie	I know you are a perfectionist but there was no need to put thatch on it.

11

Have You Ever Noticed?

Have you ever noticed that ...

When you arrive on time the teacher's always late?

It never rains while you are in the classroom but always starts when you leave school?

Whenever your dad offers to help with your homework you get bad marks?

If you are really ill adults think you are faking?

They always have your favourite school dinners on the day you are off school?

The best TV programmes come on when you have a lot of homework that must be done?

The subjects you revise for an examination are never included in the exam paper?

The school cook usually has her lunch at the café around the corner?

Spot the Space Invader

This little character is an escapee from a Space Invaders video game.

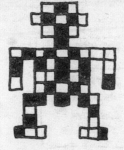

Below are a number of his friends. They all look rather similar, but in fact only one is identical to the character at the top of the page. Can you spot which one it is?

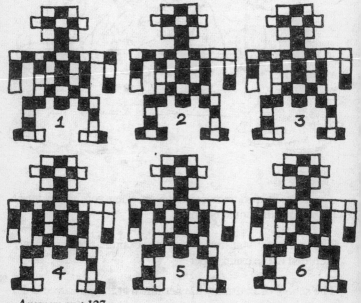

Answers on p127

Going Round and Round

Some numbers are called "circular numbers". One such is 142857. You will see why it is "circular" when you start multiplying it by other numbers as follows:

$$142857 \times 1 = 142857$$
$$\times 4 = 428571$$
$$\times 2 = 285714$$
$$\times 6 = 857142$$
$$\times 3 = 571428$$
$$\times 5 = 714285$$

As you can see, the number simply moves along one place each time. The digit that was at the start of the previous answer is then tagged on to the end. So each answer is made up of the same numbers and they are all in the same circular sequence.

It only works when the number is multiplied by the numbers from one to six. If you multiply by seven the system doesn't work. You do, however, get quite a surprising answer – 999999. Strange, isn't it?

15

10 − 1 = 1

Place seven matches on the table, as in the illustration below, to form the sum 10 − 1 = 1. By moving just one match can you make a correct sum?

Answers on p127

A Flower for the Teacher

If you have a lady teacher she might appreciate it if you took her a nice flower.

Ask your parents if you can pick one from your garden to take to school. When you say you are taking it for your teacher they will think you have gone soft in the head. On the way to school break the stem in half.

Smile sweetly as you approach the teacher with the flower in your hand. Hold the flower at the break in the stem so it looks complete. Say, "I've brought this pretty flower for you, Miss." Ignore your mates, who are cringing at the way you are making up to the teacher, for they will shortly get quite a surprise.

The teacher should then say, "Thank you, dear," and pat you on the head (so that is why you have got a flat head!). Make sure she takes the bottom half of the stem. You now just walk away with the top half still bearing the flower – much to your teacher's surprise.

After pulling this prank it is advisable to leave the country for a while.

Books for Whizzkids

Here are some of the books that can be found in the Whizz-kid's school library:

BULLETS ARE FLYING by Rick O'Shea
LOTS OF SUMS by Adam Up
IT'S RAINING AGAIN by A. Pauline Whether
HOUSEMAID'S AILMENT by Denise R. Saw
THE NARROW STREET by Ali Weigh
WALKING ON THE SPOT by Mark Thyme
RING FOR LUNCH by Deana Bell
HOW TO BE A DETECTIVE by Ivor Clue
WILL THE MAIL GO? by Ezra Post
PAMPERED by Mollie Coddle

Impossible Juggling

Show your friends a long pencil (if you haven't got any friends you can always try showing it to your enemies). Place one end of the pencil on your outstretched forefinger and then let go with the other hand. The pencil will naturally fall to the floor. Do this a few more times and sooner or later someone will ask what you are up to. "I am just trying to balance this pencil on my finger," you reply innocently. "But that's absolutely impossible," everyone will say.

Now you spring your trap. Say, "I bet you I can support this pencil on my right forefinger. I will not touch any other part of the pencil, either with my other hand or with any part of my body. And I will not get anyone else to touch it either. In spite of this I bet I can keep the pencil in a horizontal position for as long as I like."

It sounds absolutely impossible but it is quite easy to win the bet. All you do is rest the other part of the pencil on the edge of a table, so your finger supports one end and the table supports the other!

Drink Up

Boast that you are the fastest drinker in the school and sooner or later someone will ask you to prove your crazy claim. This is how you do it.

Place five large glasses of liquid on the table in front of you and five small glasses in front of your challenger. State that you can drink your five before your friend can drink his. You are not allowed to touch any of his glasses, he must not touch any of yours, and no one else can touch them.

On your marks, get set, go! Drink the first of your glasses as quickly as you can. Now tip the empty glass over the last full small glass. As your opponent cannot touch any of your glasses he is unable to get at his last glass and you can finish drinking at your leisure.

If you think you will not be able to drink the first large glass before your friend reaches his last glass, just drink half of it and pour the rest into each of the other four glasses.

Go to the Top in Human Biology

If you want to be top of the class in human biology, use some of these amazing facts in your next essay.

Your skin has about thirty different layers but even so it is only just over a millimetre thick. An adult person has nearly two square metres of skin which, if placed on some scales, would weigh less than 200 grammes.

People with blond hair have an average of 140,000 hairs on their head. People with brown have 109,000. Those with black hair have around 108,000, and people with red hair come bottom of the table with an average of only 90,000 hairs on their head.

Blonde

Brown

RED

People with red hair come bottom of the table

The correct name for a "yawn" is "an involuntary mandibular depression and maximum elevation which exposes the nasopharynx".

You blink several hundred times a day, which means that your eyes are closed for about half an hour each day.

If your nerves were stretched out end to end they would go round the world several times. What a nerve!

There are over five hundred muscles in your body.

A small muscle in the upper lip has the longest name of all the muscles. It is the *levator labii superioris aleoquae nasi*.

An adult person normally walks about 19,000 steps a day. Measured over a lifetime this gives a total of about 62,000 miles, the equivalent of walking around the world two and a half times!

The muscles of the jaw can exert a pressure of 225 kilograms – that's about the weight of three adult chimpanzees. Nobody's going to make a monkey out of you!

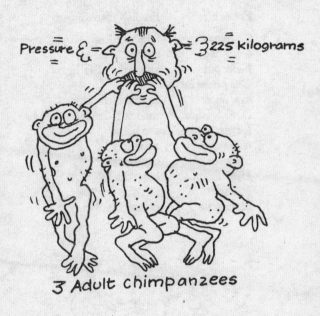

Pressure = 225 kilograms

3 Adult chimpanzees

Many people think that the "funny bone" is so called because of the tingling sensation that is felt when it is knocked, but this is not the case. The correct name for this bone that runs from the shoulder down to the elbow is the humerus! Because this sounds like "humorous", medical students nicknamed it "the funny bone". What a laugh!

Fractured French

If you go on a school trip to a foreign country it is a good idea to learn at least a litle bit of the language. Whizzkids don't usually bother to do this, for many words in European languages are similar to English and it is possible to guess their meanings. But watch out! It doesn't work every time, as you can see from these translations devised by a Whizzkid.

French	English translation
Champagne	fake window
Entre chat	entry for the cat
Faux pas	an enemy of father
Une plume de mon oncle	a monocled plum
Dans le main	the main dance
La mer	she horse
Non merci	no mercy
S'il vous plaît	silver plate
Deux enfants	baby ducks
Poisson blanquette	poison blanket

Deux enfants

Catch Your Maths Teacher

Here is a good way to catch your arithmetic teacher. After that you can try the same stunt on your friends.

Write the sum below on a postcard. Write the numbers as large as you can with the largest possible gap between each row of figures.

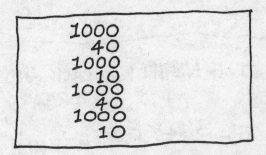

Show the card to your teacher or a friend. If your teacher is your friend then you can show it to both at the same time! When you first show the card use your hand or another card to cover up all the figures except the top row.

Tell your victim (especially if his name Vic or Tim) that you are going to test his (or her) ability to do a reasonably simple addition sum. Move your hand down to reveal a line at a time and ask your teacher to add the numbers as you move down the column.

Before reading any further add up the figures yourself. One thousand plus forty is one thousand and forty; plus one thousand is two thousand and forty, plus ten is two thousand and fifty; and so on.

Was your answer 5,000? That is the answer most people will get. It is more than likely that your maths teacher will get it wrong also. If you do the addition sum carefully you will find the correct answer is 4,100.

Can I Have Your Autograph?

When Whizzkids are asked to sign their name in an auto-graph book they usually write something witty as well. Here are some of the Whizzkids' rhymes and signatures spotted in autograph books all over the world (well, actually the result of ten minutes' research in Nicola Snodsworth's autograph book when she wasn't looking).

THE NIGHT WAS DARK AND
DREARY,
THE BILLY GOAT WAS BLIND.
HE WALKED INTO A BARBED
WIRE FENCE,
AND SCRATCHED HIS —
NEVER YOU MIND
Claude Bottom.

Roses are red,
Violets are blue,
Sugar is sweet,
and so are you.

Ugh!
signed,

Honey Treet.
× × ➤❤ × ×

As you look in this book,
Your face wears a frown,
to find that some stupid kid,
Has written upside down;
Love from
Topsy Turvy

Computerised Circles

Copy the numbered circles shown on pages 30 and 31 on to a sheet of paper. You may find it easier to get a local stationer to photocopy the pages for you. It will only cost a few pence.

Show the circles to a friend and point out that not even a genius like you could possibly remember all the numbers shown. He (or she) will probably not agree that you are a genius (although he might change his mind after you have shown him this), but he will agree that remembering all the numbered circles would be very difficult.

Ask him to place five small coins, or game counters, on any part of the sheet so that they form one or other of the patterns shown below. Turn away while he is doing this. Then announce that you can calculate the total of the numbers hidden by the coins.

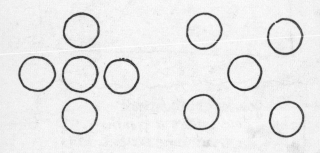

Call out the number 110. When your friend adds the numbers he will be astounded to find that you are absolutely right! In fact you will always be right, for no matter where the coins are placed, provided they are in one of the formations shown, the hidden numbers will always total 110.

As the total is always the same you cannot repeat this stunt in front of the same people, but there are a couple more tricks you can do with these computerised circles.

Give your victim one more coin and have the six coins placed consecutively anywhere on the circles in a straight line (for all you dunderheads, consecutively means next to one another – but don't worry, the author had to look it up in a dictionary before he knew what it meant). The straight line can be horizontal, vertical or diagonal. Once again you should have your back turned while this is being done.

Turn round again and secretly count five circles in a straight line from either of the end coins. In your head add the total of the numbers in the fifth circle to 110. The answer you get, if you have added correctly, will be the total of all the numbers in the circles hidden by the coins. This can be repeated if you wish.

Now turn your back again for the final demonstration of your fantastic computer-like brain. Ask your victim to place just one of the coins on any circle he or she wishes. When you turn back again, secretly count to the fifth circle in a straight line in any direction from the coin. The numbers in the circle will add up to the same total as the numbers in the hidden circle.

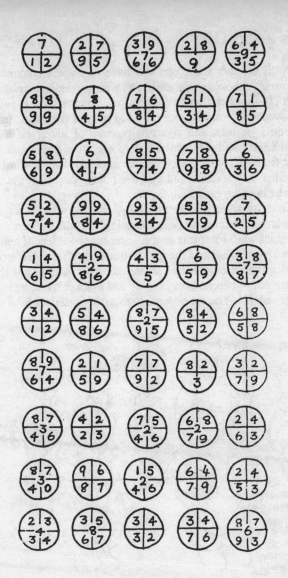

31

It's a Rip-Off

To pull off this stunt you will have to stage a convincing argument (shouldn't be difficult) with a friend or relative, with some other friends looking on. Eventually you get so annoyed that you ask your friend to remove his tie and undo the cuff buttons and top two buttons of his shirt. Your "audience" will be astonished to see him obey your instructions. They will be even more astonished when you grab his shirt by the collar and pull it off him, in spite of the fact that he is still wearing a jacket!

To do this you will first have to find a friend who is game for a laugh. Before you begin "arguing" he puts his shirt on in a special way. First it is draped over his shoulders. Then he does up the collar and the first button at the front. His wrists go through the openings above the cuffs, which are then buttoned. When he puts on a tie and a jacket the shirt looks quite normal. You are now ready to go through your little act!

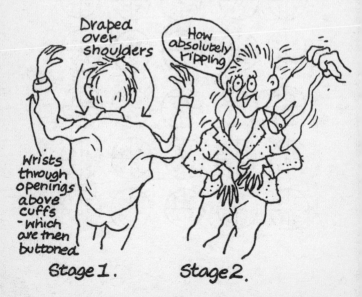

Draped over shoulders

How absolutely ripping

Wrists through openings above cuffs – which are then buttoned

Stage 1.

Stage 2.

Love Letter

Algernon Entwhistle was always getting told off for chasing the girls. One day the arithmetic teacher caught him passing a note to Thelma Sidebottom. The teacher grabbed the note but he could not tell Algernon off for there were just a few numbers written on it.

Although the teacher did not realise it, the paper did carry a cheeky message. Can you read what it says?

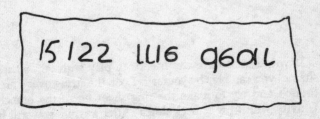

Answers on p127

Give Us a Ring

This is a great game you can play at school during break time or during the school holidays. It is not recommended that you play it in class as your teacher might take it away to play in the staff room.

It is quite simple, so making it will not tax your tiny brain too much. All you need is a long piece of string or rope and a ring or small tube. Tie the rope into a loop and place the ring over the rope.

You hold one end of the loop, and a friend holds the other. Quickly open out the loop at your end and the ring will shoot to the other end of the rope. The person at the other end opens his loop to make the ring return. The object of the game is to make the ring return before it hits your hands. If it does, you shout, "*'?*/"?" (or words to that effect). You also lose a point.

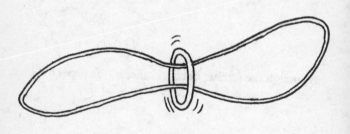

If you do not have any friends to play with (ah, what a shame) you can play by yourself. Loop the string over a high branch and try to make the ring shoot up to the branch. Gravity will bring it back down. After a while you will be exhausted, you will have developed biceps like King Kong, and the branch will break and fall on your head. Great fun!

Confusing Cubes

Take a look at the picture on this page and see if you can say how many cubes are in it.

You will come up with one of two answers depending on which way you look at the picture. If you look at the white squares and imagine them as the top of the cubes your answer will be seven. But if you concentrate on the black squares and regard them as the bottom of the cubes your answer will be eight.

You could show this picture to one of your teachers, and ask him or her how many cubes there are. If he or she says eight, you can prove that there are really seven. And if the teacher says seven, you can prove that there are eight. Confusing, isn't it?

Project Topics

Many teachers are keen on their pupils doing projects on a wide variety of subjects. At first sight a project seems like a lot of hard work. True, there is work to be done, but if you approach your project in the right way you will find, much to your surprise, that you actually want to find out more.

From a learning point of view project work is much better than the pupil (that's you) simply reading from a book or sitting in class while the teacher drones on and on, and on, and on, and on, and . . . You will learn a lot more if you are actively engaged in finding out about a subject for yourself.

The choice of subject is probably the most important part of any project. In many cases you will not have any choice, for the teacher will tell you what subject you have to cover. If you have a free choice pick a subject in which you are already interested, one that you would like to know about, or one that has some connection with a subject in which you are already interested. Think carefully before making your final choice. You should also try to pick a subject on which you can be certain of obtaining information. At the same time try to pick something that no one else is likely to choose.

It is a good idea, especially in the initial stages, to write the subject down in a bubble (not a soap bubble) then work from the centre, writing down any connected thoughts that come to you. This may sound rather complicated so let's try an example. Let's suppose that the subject you want to cover is Fire. First write down the word "fire" in a bubble, like this:

Now start thinking about fire (or whatever your subject is) and note down everything you can. Fire? How was it discovered? Great fires; forest fires; fire-fighting. Your plan will begin to look something like this:

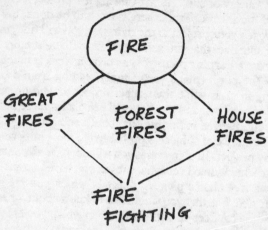

Continue jotting down all the ideas you can. Look at the headings you have made and see if they spark off (joke) any further ideas. Great fires? Can you think of any great fires in history? The Fire of London comes to mind but was there also a big fire in Chicago – or was it San Francisco, or was it both? Jot it down, you can check it later.

You will be surprised how many ideas come to you, even with a subject you do not know very well. In fact your chart may even get quite complicated. If it gets as big as the one shown below you may decide not to cover the whole subject after all but concentrate (if you are capable of concentrating) on just one part of it. So, instead of studying fire you pick just fire-fighting, for example.

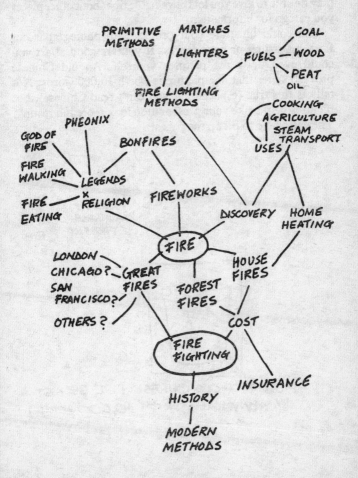

The next step is to start looking for information about your chosen topic. There are many sources you can use. Among them are the local library, museums, newspapers, magazines, radio, television, and companies.

Make full use of your library and tell the librarian what you are doing. Librarians are very helpful if you show an interest in something. They can tell you what books are available and may be able to give you lots of valuable tips about other places you can go for information.

You could illustrate your project with photographs cut from magazines or newspapers. If you are good at art you could even draw the pictures yourself. An old Chinese proverb states that one picture is worth 10,000 words. Not only is this true (especially if you can't read Chinese), but pictures help make your presentation look more interesting. They also help to fill up the pages!

ANCIENT
CHINESE
FIREFLY

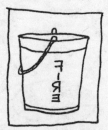

PICTURE OF OLD CHINESE FIRE BUCKET
(Very valuable—Worth 10,000 words)

Do not be afraid to write to businesses for information. They can provide you with useful material about your selected subject. All large companies have a publicity or sales promotion manager, part of whose job is to provide printed information about the firm's products.

Keep a look out for radio and television programmes about your chosen subject. You will be able to get a lot of information from them.

Try to make your written work as original as you can. It is very easy to just copy chunks from newspapers, books and magazines, but in many cases this just results in a boring series of bits and pieces all written in different styles. Put things in your own words as much as possible.

Try to keep your project notes as neat as you possibly can. Not only will neatness gain you extra marks but it will also enable you and your teacher to read the information much more easily. If the whole project is presented in an orderly manner it becomes more obvious that you have put a lot of time and effort into it. You never know, you may even get top marks!

you never know, you might even get to the top

In the Dining Room

These two pictures of a typical school dining room appear to be the same but they are not. There are ten differences between the two pictures. Can you find them?

Answers on p127

Be a Whizzkid at Art

Test your ability as an artist by trying to identify each of these pictures. When you have done that, or after you have cheated by looking at the answers on page 127, try them out on your art teacher.

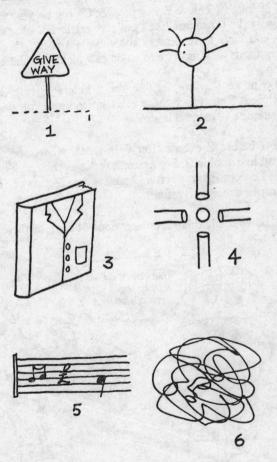

How Two Spel Kerreckly

Spelling correctly can be quite a problem at times. The trouble is that there are very few rules that can be applied to English spelling. And what rules there are usually have many exceptions to them.

The rule "I before E except after C" can be very useful. This works for words like "piece", "retrieve", and "field", but you have to remember there are words like "leisure", "neighbour", "height" and so on to which the rules do not apply.

To make it more reliable the I before E rule can be modified. Remember these rules instead and you may not make quite so many mistakes.

a) I before E except after C in words where the vowels sound like double E. For example: relieve, thief, grieve.

b) I before E except after C, unless the C forms a CH. For example: achieve, chieftain.

But be warned, there are exceptions of both of these rules too!

44

Exceptions to the rules can make spelling a frustrating business. But as Whizzkids are born to overcome problems, here are a few tips you can try to improve your spelling:

1. Make up a short sentence that helps remind you of the correct spelling. Let's take a look at the words "grammar" and believe. Do not *mar* your English with bad gram*mar*; Never be*lie*ve a *lie*.

I've been told you can't spell

Never believe a lie

2. Where you have words that sound the same but are spelled differently you really only have to learn one to know the spelling of both. Using the sentence technique on the words "stationery/stationary" and "principal/principle" you might come up with something like this. A station*er* sells station*ery*; The princi*pal* should be your *pal*.

3. Sometimes it is possible to remember the spelling of a word because the letters can be given a certain rhythm:

Mississippi	M-I-double S I-double S I-double P I
Repetition	RE-PE TI-TI ON

If nun of these tecknikes are sootible for yu, yu will have to go on spelling rongly or think up sum speshul teknikes of yur own.

Octagon Perplexer

Here is a difficult problem for your arithmetic teacher. Hand her a square of paper and challenge her to cut a regular octagon from it. She will just be about to get out her pencil, ruler and compasses when you quietly inform her that she is not allowed any of them. Scissors are the only things she can use. Like many puzzles, this looks impossible but is easy when you know the trick.

Get a square piece of paper and follow these instructions. First fold the paper in half one way by folding the edge AF on to CH. Open out the paper and then fold it in half the other way – folding AC on to FH. These folds will give you the central points on each side. These central points are marked B, D, E and G in the drawing.

The next step is to use the central points as markers so that you can fold down each corner to form the square BEDG. Open up the paper once again. Now fold AB on to the line BD. Open the paper and then fold AD on to the same line.

This will give you the central point I in the top left-hand corner as shown in the illustration. Do exactly the same with the other three corners and the octagon will be clearly marked ready for you to cut it out.

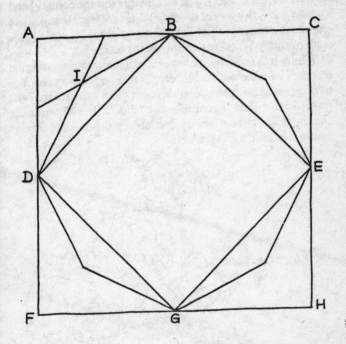

Nota Bene

Ab initio (from the beginning) of time teachers, *ex officia* (by virtue of their position), have persecuted pupils *ad nauseum* (to a sickening degree). But *au contraire* (on the contary) and *exempli gratia* (by way of example) there are ways that you can change the *status quo* (no, it's not a pop group, it means "the state of things") and get one up on the teachers.

Whilst it is *infra dig* (below one's dignity) to creep around teachers *ad infinitum* (to infinity, or forever), it is a good idea to impress them when possible to get good marks. One *bona fide* (which means "genuine" – not "Fido's" bone") way to do this is to show how brainy you are by using some foreign phrases in essays and projects.

Infra dig.
(lots of spade work)

Fido

genuine

bona fide
(Fido's bone)

It is quite permissible to write *hors de combat* for "no longer in a condition to fight" (not "horse of war"), *aide de camp* (not Ada Camp, the canteen lady) which means "an officer who carries messages for a general" (or "a secretary"), or *double entendre* (which doesn't mean "double doors" but refers to a word or phrase that has a double meaning) to show how brilliant you are.

There are lots of other words and phrases you can use as well. If you look at the back of a good dictionary you will find a whole list from Latin, Greek and modern languages that can be used as if they were English. Learn some of them and your teachers will think you are a genius (if they do not think it already).

Nota Bene (note well) therefore that it can be useful to use foreign phrases. An essay containing such phrases could prove to be your *pièce de resistance* (the best you ever do). If you go wrong you can always say it was a *lapsus calami* (slip of the pen) or a *lapsus memoriae* (slip of the memory). In oral tests any mistake can be attributed to a *lapsus linguae* (a slip of the tongue). Should you make a mistake you can always console yourself with the thought that *errare est humanum* (to make mistakes is human).

Bonne Chance!

lapsus linguae
(slip of the tongue)

lapsus calami →
(slip of the pen)

Knickers

lapsus
bananae —— (slip of the banana skin)

49

Odd Man Out - Naturally

Can you say which is the "odd man out" in each of these lists of things from nature?

1. Penguin, Ostrich, Peacock, Rhea, Emu, Cassowary.

2. Koala, Sun, Spectacled, Brown, Polar, Kodiak, Honey-pot.

3. Hippopotamus, Armadillo, Giraffe, Zebra, Okapi.

4. Eagle, Buzzard, Sparrowhawk, Kestrel, Pheasant, Harrier, Barn Owl, Merlin.

5. Alligator, Duck-billed Platypus, Frog, Ant, Mouse.

6. Oak, Beech, Cypress, Elm, Horse Chestnut.

7. Devon Rex, Siamese, Burmese, Foreign Lilac, Adder, Manx.

8. Tigar, Lion, Cuscus, Leopard, Lynx, Cougar.

9. Marmot, Cobra, Python, Anaconda, Viper, Boomslang.

MARMITE POT   MARMOT

Answers on p127

Numbered Thoughts

Think of any number between 1 and 50 and write it down on a piece of paper. Fold the paper and hand it to a friend for safe keeping. let us assume that the number you wrote down was 23.

Mentally subtract that number from 99 (it is as well to choose a number that will make this sum easy for you to do in your head). In our example the answer you will get will be 76. Remember this for the moment.

Ask your friend to think of any number between 50 and 100. We will assume that he picks 73. Ask him to now add 76 (the number you obtained earlier) to his number. His answer in this instance will be 149.

Now tell him to cross of the first digit of his answer and add it to the remaining digits. (So he will cross of the 1 and add it to the 49 to get the answer 50). The next thing he has to do is take that answer away from the number he first thought of (73 – 50 = 23).

Now he opens the piece of paper you gave him earlier and he will be absolutely flabbergasted, open mouthed, stupified, awestruck, dumbfounded, thunderstruck and completely underwhelmed at your amazing ability to predict the future.

Now You See It, Now You Don't

Get a piece of black card and cover it with wax. The easiest way to do this is to rub an ordinary wax candle all over the card. You now need a sheet of greaseproof paper (ask your mum if she has got any in the kitchen). Put the greaseproof paper on top of the waxed card. Use sticky tape on the underside of the card to keep the greaseproof paper in place.

Get a long, narrow strip of card and place it across the top of the greaseproof paper as shown in the drawings. This strip should be longer than the width of your magic slate. Over the top of the magic slate place a sheet of clear, sticky-backed plastic. This should be long enough so that the plastic can be folded over each end and stuck to the back of the card.

Your magic slate is now complete. Write something on the top plastic and the writing can be read quite easily. When you push the cardboard strip along to the end of the slate the writing will be erased. You will be able to use the writing surface over and over again. After a while you may have to lift up the plastic and the greaseproof paper to rewax the card.

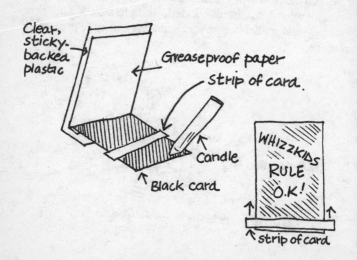

Clear, sticky-backed plastic

Greaseproof paper

Strip of card.

Candle

Black card

WHIZZKIDS RULE O.K!

strip of card

Be a V.I.P.

The initials V.I.P. do not stand for Virtually Intelligent Pupil or Vulgar Idiotic Pupil. V.I.P. is an abbreviation for Very Important Person.

Here is a good way to impress your friends that you are a V.I.P. All you have to do is to say "Hello" to someone in the street. When your friends ask, "Who was that?" you reply as casually as you can, "Oh, that was the Lord Mayor, we're great pals." Do not however, fall into the trap of pretending that everyone you speak to is the Lord Mayor or your friends will soon catch on to your dodge. Have a few more titles ready, such as Lord of the Local Manor, my friend the Duke of Sniggleswick, or Admiral of the Fleet.

Surprisingly enough, most people will return your greeting. Because V.I.P.s meet lots of people they cannot remember them all. If your luck is really in, the person you greet may even stop and ask you how you are keeping and if your parents are well. That should get your friends fuming with jealousy.

Of course, there will be some who will tell you to clear off. If this happens you just turn to your friend and say, "He (or she) is always a misery until he wants my advice on something."

Do It Yourshelf

If you've got lots of books and no bookshelf you can make one quite easily. All you need are some clean house bricks and a few planks of wood.

Place four bricks in the corner of the room. Put the same number of bricks a short distance away and then rest the first plank on the two piles. Build up a few more bricks and put on the next plank. Continue building in this manner until you have the number of shelves you need.

Because the bricks are not cemented together you must be careful how you pile them up. It is a good idea to build this bookcase in a recess as the walls will then give the support needed. Under no circumstances build the shelves higher than about one metre as they may topple.

Where do you get the things needed for this brick bookshelf? Well, to get the bricks you can knock down the house next door, ask your dad, or buy them from a builder. Don't know where to get the wood? Use your head.

SHELF FOR PUTTING THINGS ON

SPACE FOR BOOKS

← BOOK WORMS
WAITING FOR BOOKS
TO WORM INTO

Keeping Dry Underwater

Did you know that it is possible for something to keep dry even though it is underwater? That may sound absolutely crazy but it can be a fact – and, what is more, you can prove it.

Show your friends an ordinary handkerchief and then bunch it up and put it into a glass tumbler. Push the handkerchief right down to the bottom of the glass so that it will not fall out when you turn the glass over.

Fill a bowl with water and then push the glass, mouth down, into the water. If you make sure you hold the glass absolutely straight you will be able to submerge the glass completely but the handkerchief will not get at all wet.

For the scientifically minded, this is due to the fact that air trapped in the glass when it is first submerged prevents any water from entering. Isn't science wonderful?

The Paper Altar

Take a rectangular sheet of paper (the exact size doesn't matter). Can you now, with only one straight cut, transform that piece of paper so it forms the shape of a church altar complete with cross and lighted candles? What? You can't do it? Well, it is really quite simple. This is all you have to do.

Fold the left corner down to meet the right edge as shown in the second illustration. Now bring the right corner down to meet the left edge in the same way.

Next fold the paper exactly in half by bringing the left edge over to meet the right edge. Now fold the right edge in to meet the left edge. In other words, you have folded the paper in half once again.

All you have to do now is make one straight cut from A to B as shown in the fifth illustration. Open out the pieces of paper and you can arrange them to form the cross and altar shown in the final picture. Although easy to do, this little puzzle is really quite impressive.

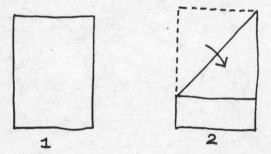

1   2

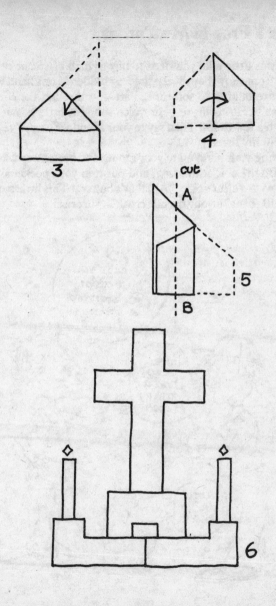

3

4

cut

A

B

5

6

I've a Frog in My Throat

For this little joke you need to buy a small plastic or rubber frog from a toy shop. Keep the frog hidden in one hand while you are talking to someone. Part way through the conversation begin to make your voice sound a little hoarse and cough a few times. Then say to your friend, "Sorry, I've got a frog in my throat."

Bring your hand up to your mouth and pretend to take out the frog. Look at the frog, and put it in your pocket as you say, with a clear voice, "Ah, that's better." This little stunt is bound to make your friends croak in surprise!

Arithmetic Exam

1. Can you take 2 from 11 and make the answer even?

2. See how quickly you can work out the answer to this multiplication sum in your head:
   1x2x3x4x5x6x7x8x9x0 =

3. If you have two coins totalling 15p and one of them is not a 5p, what are the two coins?

4. Add 4 to 193 and make the answer total less than 20.

5. Can you draw 8 triangles with just 6 straight lines?

6. How many triangles are there in this pentagram?

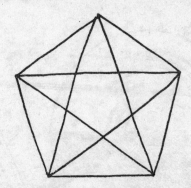

7. If 1 = orange, 2 = turquoise, and 3 = tangerine, what do 4 and 5 equal?

8. What maths symbol can be placed between the numbers 2 and 3 to make a number larger than 2 but less than 3?

Answers on p127

Incredible Video Disc

Although most video recorders use magnetic tape there is also a system that uses a video disc. This disc is rather like an ordinary gramophone record except that it produces pictures and sound instead of sound only. But you do not need a video recorder to try out the Whizzkid's video disc. Admittedly, it will not produce pictures – but it can create colour where no colour exists.

First you will have to copy the disc shown below – complete with black shading – on to a sheet of card. Make a hole in the centre of the card so you can put it on to a record player. If you do not have a record player push a pencil through the centre to make a top like the one in the picture.

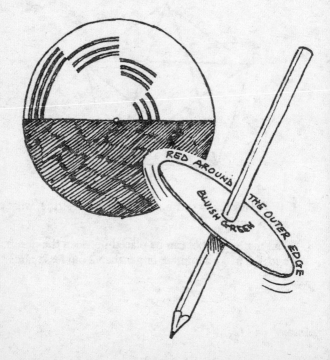

Now switch on the record player, or spin the top, and the disc will appear to be red around the outer edge and bluish-green in the centre. If you reverse the direction of the spin (which you can do with the top but not with the record player) the position of the colours is also reversed.

Why not show it to your science teacher? At the same time you can tell him that this remarkable video disc was invented by Charles Benham in 1894, long before televisions and video recorders where even thought of. That should earn you an extra mark or two in your next science test!

Loony Lingo

Here are some silly definitions that you are unlikely to find in a normal dictionary.

ARTERY – a place where you can buy paintings

BARBECUE – people lining up for a haircut

BIG GAME HUNTER – a man who loses his way to a football match

CANNIBAL – someone who is feeling fed up with people

CROWBAR – a place where crows go to drink

CROWBAR

CYCLONE – going for a bike ride by yourself

DANCING – the art of pulling your feet away faster than your partner can step on them

ETC. – an abbreviation used to make the teacher believe you know more than you really do

EUROPE – where everyone drives on the wrong side of the road

FREE SPEECH – when you use someone else's telephone

GOSSIP – someone with a good sense of rumour

HATCHET – what a bird tries to do when it sits on an egg

HATCHET

KNAPSACK – a sleeping bag

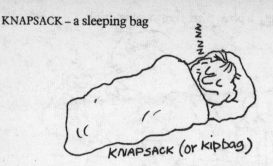

KNAPSACK (or kipbag)

MANNERS – learning to yawn with your mouth closed

RELIEF – what trees do each spring

SCHOOL SPIRIT – a ghost that haunts the school

SOURPUSS – a cat that has swallowed a lemon

TORTOISE – what our teacher did

TORTOISE

WIND – air in a hurry

WITCHCRAFT – a flying broomstick

Magic Money

If your friends would like a chance to make some money for nothing, show them this trick.

You will need a £5 note (if you are not that rich, a £1 note will do). You also need four slips of paper the same size as the £5, and five envelopes. Put the £5 in one of the envelopes and seal it down. Mark this envelope with a small pencil dot in one corner so you know which one it is. Put the slips of paper in the other envelopes and seal them. You are now ready.

Mark the envelope with a small pencil dot

Show the envelopes to your friends and explain that one of them contains a £5 note and you are going to give them a chance to win it. Hand the envelopes to someone to mix them up. When you get them back you apparently mix them up a little more. What you are really doing is looking for the marked envelope (with the £5 inside). Continue mixing the envelopes until you have got the marked one second from the top of the pile.

Hand the envelopes to a spectator and tell him (or her) to spell the word MONEY, transferring one envelope from the top to the bottom of the pile as she calls out each letter. She is to keep the envelope that falls on the letter Y.

The first spectator then hands the envelopes to a second person who does exactly the same. Two other people also have a go and the last remaining envelope is handed to you. To make your audience laugh at this point you can do the spelling routine as well – as have only one envelope it looks rather funny.

Each spectator opens his or her envelope, but all they contain are slips of paper (you could write some funny remarks on the slips like, "That's the easiest £5 you never earned!", or "Easy come, easy go!"). When you open your envelope it contains the £5. "It must be magic," you tell your audience.

Although this trick works automatically you should try it out in private first to make sure you understand the instructions. It could prove rather expensive if you made a mistake and one of the spectators got the £5 instead of you!

It could prove rather expensive . . . . . .

Finger Nail

Get an adult to bend a nail in a vice into the shape shown below. The bend should be large enough to go around one of your fingers.

Make yourself a finger ring out of cardboard and attach the nail to the ring. Possibly the easiest way to do this is to use a needle and thread and sew the two together.

Place the ring, complete with nail, on your finger and get a friend to wind a bandage around it to hide the cardboard. A few drops of glue placed on the bandage at intervals will help to hold the whole thing in place. The winding of the bandage should not be too tight for you need to be able to slip it on and off your finger.

Use some red ink or a red felt pen to stain the bandage near the nail. When you put the completed bandage on, it looks as if there is a nail going straight through your finger. Put it on and say to a teacher: "I am sorry but I can't do any writing today – I have had a slight accident." Show him the finger and get ready to run for your life – just in case the teacher does not approve of your sense of humour!

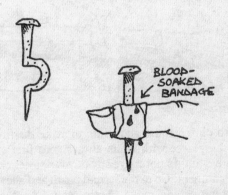

BLOOD-SOAKED BANDAGE

Prove You are a Chess Master

Chess masters often demonstrate their skill by playing against several players at once. Being a Whizzkid you can do the same. You can win or draw at least half the games you play using the diabolical technique about to be described. You don't know how to play chess? Never mind – with this system you don't need to know how!

Challenge four chess players to a game at the same time. Get them to sit far enough apart so they cannot see what is taking place on the other boards. Imagine the four players as numbers 1, 2, 3, and 4. Players 1 and 2 have white pieces, players 3 and 4 have black pieces. In other words, you play with the black pieces on the first two games, and with the white pieces on the other two games.

A diabolical Whizzkid Chess Master

Go to player 1 and allow him to make the first move (In chess the player with white always goes first). Remember that move but do not move any of your pieces on that board for the moment. Go to the second board and allow player 2 to make his opening move. Again, you do not respond but simply remember the move.

Now move across to board three. As you have the white pieces it is up to you to make the first move. Remember the opening move made by player 1? That is the first move you make on board three.

Move to board four, where you make the same opening move as player 2 did.

Go back to board three and wait for the player there to move one of his black pieces in response to your opening move. Remember that move. Do not respond but casually walk back to board four.

Do not respond, but walk casually back to board 4.

When player 4 has moved, go back to board one. Here you now make your second move of that game, repeating the move made by player 3. On board two you make the move remembered from board four.

After players 1 and 2 have responded you then wander over to board three and four and make exactly the same moves. Wait for players 3 and 4 to make their moves and then go and make exactly the same moves on boards one and two. Continue in this fashion until all four games are completed.

Although the players will not realise it, you are not taking part in the games at all. You are really making player 1 play against 3, and player 2 against 4. All you are doing is acting as a sort of messenger boy, carrying the moves between the boards. You are the only person who is not playing!

How to Read Faster

If you do a lot of reading you can save quite a lot of time by increasing your reading speed. All it takes is a little practice.

To find out your present reading speed have a friend time you reading for one minute. Now count the number of words you have read. If it is less than 500 you can most definitely improve upon that speed. There is no reason why you should not be able to read 500 or even 750 words a minute. At such speeds you are not reading every word – you receive only the gist of information before you. Because of this you will find that you have to vary your speed according to the type of material you are reading. Something that is technical or difficult to follow will have to be read much more slowly than a story.

Try running your finger along beneath each line of print as you read. No doubt you were discouraged from doing this when you first started to read but it is not really a bad habit. At that time you were probably pointing to each word individually. This time you must move your finger along at a steady pace without stopping. Gradually increase the speed at which you move your finger and your reading speed will increase at the same time. Try not to go too fast too quickly. Build up your speed gradually and you will achieve much better results.

"gradually increase the speed you move your finger"

Your eyes do not run smoothly over a page as you read. Watch the eyes of a reader carefully and you will see that they go across a line of print in a series of hops, stopping every so often. It is during these stops that the eyes are actually taking in the words. Slow readers tend to stop a lot. This is probably because they are looking at each and every word in the line. Faster readers stop less often and take in several words at each stop. This is obviously the technique to learn if you wish to improve your reading speed.

Anyone seen my eyes?

Your eyes go along a line of print in a series of hops . . .

The easiest way to learn this is to practise with a newspaper as the columns are usually fairly narrow. Draw a line right down the centre of one column. Now try to read each line, not by moving the eyes from side to side each time, but only looking at the region of the central line you have drawn. You may find it a little strange at first, but persevere and after only a short amount of practice you should find that your eyes are taking in a complete line at a time. At first you may find that you cannot fully understand what you are reading but this will come in time. If you think you are trying to take in too much try drawing two lines down the column so you only have to look at half the column each time. After a bit of practice you should find that you can do away with the pencilled lines, just running your eyes down an imaginary central line, and that you can understand what you are reading just as well as you did when you read much more slowly.

One thing you must avoid if you want to improve your reading speed is saying the words to yourself. This will slow down your reading and you will find the newspaper technique impossible to practise. Try to see the general sense of a phrase or group of words. It may not be easy but it can be done. Using the newspaper will help.

Another thing you must avoid at all costs is the habit of going back on what you have already read. If you are trying to speed up it is silly to read everything twice.

Reading at speed is of no use if you lose the sense of what you are reading. It is therefore worthwhile to stop every so often during your practice sessions and test your understanding of what you have just read.

As your reading speeds increase you will find that you want to read more and more. Reading can be done in many odd moments for paperbacks are easily carried in the pocket or bag to be read at any time. It is amazing how much reading you can get through in odd five-minute sessions snatched here and there.

Reading can be done in many odd moments

English Multiple Choice

Only one of the three definitions given for each word below is correct. Test your knowledge of English and see if you know which is the correct meaning in each case.

1. *Incognito*
a) A mechanical device used in computers.
b) An Italian boatman.
c) In disguise or under an assumed name.

2. *Revere*
a) To regard with high respect.
b) The south coast of France.
c) To live in a cave.

Mr. A.N. OTHER.
(An ASSUMED NAME)

And I'm under it

4. *Laburnum*
a) A laboratory fire.
b) A small tree.
c) A political party.

3. *Kedgeree*
a) Tool used for cutting hedges.
b) Net used by Chinese fishermen.
c) A meal of rice and other ingedients.

5. *Filigree*
a) A lady's blouse.
b) To argue loudly.
c) Type of ornamental work.

Velly fishy net

6. *Punnet*
a) A small pun.
b) A small basket.
c) A small boat.

7. *Fandango*
a) A Spanish dance.
b) A South American dog.
c) An Italian cake.

8. *Conflagration*
a) A group of people in church.
b) A large fire.
c) An uncontrollable riot.

A South American Dog

9. *Nasturtium*
a) Nuclear waste.
b) An insult.
c) A plant.

10. *Tintinnabulation*
a) The tinkling sound of bells.
b) A process of dyeing material.
c) Ancient method of crop spraying.

11. *Procrastinate*
a) A flower of the daisy family.
b) A Roman magistrate.
c) To put off action.

12. *Fustanella*
a) A wooden settee.
b) A Greek kilt.
c) Place where cheese is stored.

A Greek kilt or place where cheese is stored

Answers on p128

The Hindu Sand Tray

The Hindus of ancient India used a small tray of sand to help them with their mathematical calculations. It was divided into squares and each square was cut diagonally to give the design shown below.

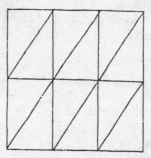

If you have trouble with multiplications the Hindu sand tray will help you. There is, however, no need to carry a tray of sand around with you! The method works equally well with pencil and paper. Let us, for example, suppose that you wish to multiply 542 by 73. First write the numbers down along the edge of the design – one number across the top and one along the side so that each digit is in line with one of the squares as shown.

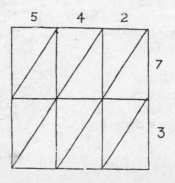

Now multiply each set of digits alongside each box. So, $7 \times 5 = 35$; $7 \times 4 = 28$; and so on. Each answer is written in the appropriate box above and below the diagonal line.

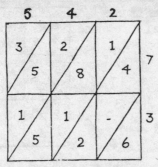

The next step is to add together the figures that appear in each diagonal line starting from the right. In the first diagonal line there is only the number 6. The second diagonal consists of $4 + 2$ which equals 6. For the third line we have $1 + 8 + 1 + 5 = 15$. As in normal addition the tens's unit of 15 is carried over into the next column. The diagram below shows the addition completed.

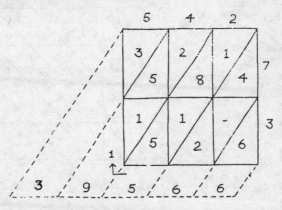

Write down the answer you have obtained and you will now know that $542 \times 73 = 39566$.

This system works equally well with larger numbers as the examples below will show.

758 x 983 = 745,114

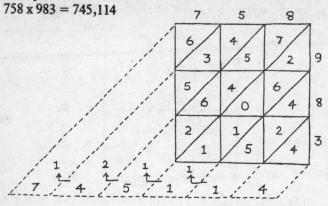

3725 x 8514 = 31,714,650

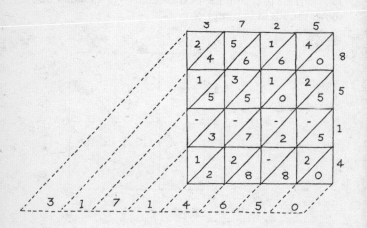

More Books for Whizzkids

Here are some more fantastic books that you may find on the shelves of a Whizzkid's library:

Hands Up!

Fold a piece of paper in half. On the top sheet draw a picture of a Whizzkid sitting in a classroom (Shame! It shouldn't be allowed) being cross examined by a teacher. On the bottom sheet draw the same picture but change the position of the Whizzkid's arm (so it is upright) and the expression on the teacher's face.

Now roll up the top sheet around a pencil.

Place the paper on a table and hold the top left corner. If you now move the pencil up and down fast you will see the Whizzkid shooting his arm in the air to answer all the questions (just like you do).

It works on a similar principle to that used to make cartoon films. Any simple movement, such as a Whizzkid running, or bouncing a ball, can be brought to life using this simple device.

Roll the top sheet round a pencil

Age of Mystery

The first *Whizzkid's Handbook* (only £5,000, and very good value for money – advert) contained a method for finding out the age of your teacher (or of anyone else for that matter). Here is another way of determining (that's a long word) someone's age.

Hand your victim – sorry, your friend – a piece of paper and a pencil. It could be a piece of paper and a pen. It could also be a piece of paper and a felt-tip pen. It could even be a torn-off piece of newspaper and a crayon – but, as you are a Whizzkid, you will have realised this already so there is no need to explain it in such detail.

Turn your back and ask your subject to do the following:

First he is to write down his age. Let us assume that he is a very old teacher and that he writes 37. Under this he is to write down his magic number. You tell him that his magic number is 90 (in fact it is always 90 but there is no need to let anyone know this).

He then has to add the first number to the second – like this:

$$\begin{array}{r} 37 \\ + \ 90 \\ \hline 127 \end{array}$$

Another method of finding out your teacher's age... Count the rings round his eyes....

Now ask him to cross out the first number on the left-hand side of his answer and then write that number underneath the total. He is then to add the two together. His paper should now look like this:

$$
\begin{array}{r}
37 \\
+\ 90 \\
\hline
127 \\
1 \\
\hline
28 \\
\hline
\end{array}
$$

Ask him for the answer he has obtained. In your head (if there is enough room) secretly add 9 to the number he gives you. The answer – in this example 37 (28 + 9) – is the person's age.

Secretly add 9 to the numbers in your head

It's a Date

Tell your friends that you are a fantastic mindreader. You even offer to prove your amazing powers.

Ask someone to remove a coin from his or her pocket. "Keep it hidden from me," you say, "and I will tell you the date." Pretend to concentrate and then call out, "July 15th" (or whatever that day's date happens to be). He expected you to call out the date on the coin and so you have caught him!

How About That!

Learn this amazing multiplication and you can use it to stun your teachers, your friends, and even your enemies.

$$15873 \times 7 = 111111$$
$$\times 14 = 222222$$
$$\times 21 = 333333$$
$$\times 28 = 444444$$
$$\times 35 = 555555$$
$$\times 42 = 666666$$
$$\times 49 = 777777$$
$$\times 56 = 888888$$
$$\times 63 = 999999$$

To remember this strange multiplication, note that all the multipliers increase by seven each time.

Lesson Mix-Up

Each set of letters below can be arranged to form the name of a school subject. Can you sort them out and say what each subject is?

1. A GREY PHOG
2. THIS ROY
3. LEG SHIN
4. IS MATCH MATE
5. TRY MICE, SH
6. SOIL DACE'S SUIT
7. RAT
8. BOY, GOIL
9. ALE BRAG
10. T. NAIL

Answers on p128

Write a Poetic Masterpiece

There used to be a time,
When poems used to rhyme,
But now that time is past,
I knew it wouldn't last.
To write a modern poem
Is quite a simple feat,
Just follow the instructions,
And write it down real neat.
On the first line put a noun,
Then two adjectives write down,
Two that describe the word,
O'wt else would be absurd.
Line three, write three verbs,
Saying what your noun can do,
On line four write a thought,
The first that comes to you.
Line five. This is the last,
So write a noun again,
Or, if you prefer,
Put down a synonym.
Just to prove it works,
Here are some super samples.
Do not just copy them,
Use them as examples.

The Wind,
Blustery, Stormy,
Puffing, blowing, roaring,
It whispers through the trees,
The wind.

Dog.
Tough yet soft,
Barks, runs, plays,
Man's best friend,
Canine.

Man.
Erect, strong,
Walks, talks, builds,
Great wonder of creation,
Homo sapiens.

Whizzkid.
Brilliant, Fantastic,
Wins, wins, wins,
Top of the Class,
Me.

Buttonholed

Ask an adult to cut a groove around one end of a long pencil (why risk cutting your fingers when there is someone else to do it for you?). Now tie a loop of string to the pencil. The loop should reach to about half-way along the length of the pencil, like the one shown (A). The purpose of the notch is to stop the string from slipping off.

Approach a friend and hold the front of his coat near a buttonhole (make sure he is your friend before you do this or you might end up with a black eye!).

Pull part of the material through the loop of string (B). Keep pulling until you can push the pencil through the buttonhole (C) or the material tears. If the material tears run like mad; if not, you can continue by pulling the string tight so that the pencil is tied securely to the buttonhole (D).

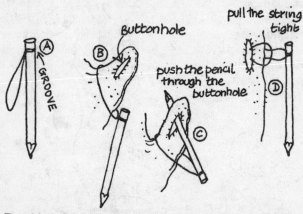

Provided that you have done this quickly (practise it in private beforehand so you can do it fast) and you do not let your friend see the movements, most people will find it impossible to remove the pencil without cutting the string or breaking the pencil. It is in fact more difficult to get off than it is to get on but it can be done by reversing the above process.

Frustrating Flexagon

In the past few years the remarkable Rubik Cube has achieved great popularity. It was invented by Erno Rubik, a Hungarian professor, and is made up of twenty-seven different coloured cubes. Twiddling with a Rubik Cube became such a craze that people developed Rubik thumb, a painful dislocation of the thumb joint caused by rotating a Cube for hours on end in the hope of solving the puzzle.

Here is a device that is simpler than the Cube but from which you can still derive a great deal of fun – and you won't develop Rubik thumb through doing it. The device is called a Hexahexaflexagon. A what? Yes, a Hexahexaflexagon!

On a long strip of paper draw nineteen equilateral triangles. That may sound difficult but there is an easy way to do it. Being a genius you know that the angles of an equilateral triangle are all 60 degrees. Simply place your strip of paper on the base line of the 60-degree angle shown in illustration 1. Mark the top and bottom of the strip where the line extends. Draw a straight line joining the two points (illustration 2) and then cut along this line with a pair of scissors.

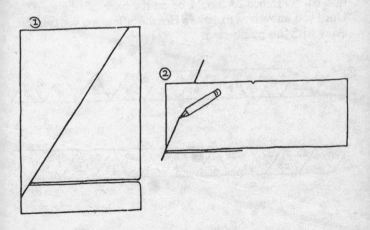

Fold the bottom corner of the strip (A) up to meet the top of the strip so that A – B is level with the top of the strip (illustration 3). Now fold B down in the same way (illustration 4) and continue in this fashion all along the strip. When the paper is opened out the creases will have formed the equilateral triangles you need.

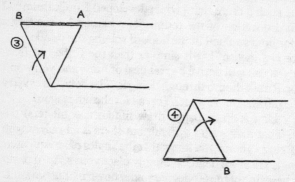

To make it easier to follow the instructions, number all the triangles from 1 to 19 as shown in illustration 5. Cut off any extra triangles. Turn the strip over from top to bottom and number the triangles on the other side from 20 to 38 (illustration 6). (Number 20 should be on the back of triangle 1). Once you know how to make a Hexahexaflexagon you can do away with this numbering.

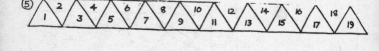

Fold triangles 1 and 2 down along the crease that separates 2 and 3. Triangle 2 should be now on top of triangle 3. The paper will look like illustration 7. Now fold 4 on to 5 and continue in this manner all the way along the strip by folding 6 on to 7, 8 on to 9, 10 on to 11, and so on. When you get to the end your paper should look like picture 8.

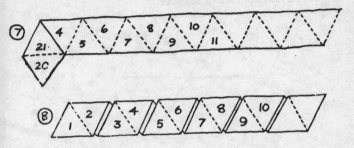

Next you must fold 25 on to 28 to arrive at illustration 9. Fold the crease between triangles 32 and 33 away from you. If you look on the other side of the strip you will be folding triangle 34 on to 31. As you do this, bring 38 in front of 22 and you should now be in the position shown in picture 10.

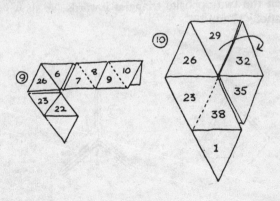

91

Open out 38 and 19 will be visible. Fold 1 up on to 18 and 20 will be visible. Put some glue on 20 and then press 19 on to it. In other words 19 and 20 are glued together.

Your Hexahexaflexagon is now complete (illustration 11). On the top surface you should have 23, 26, 29, 32, 35 and 38. Colour all these red. On the other side you will have 21, 24, 27, 30, 33 and 36. Colour these blue.

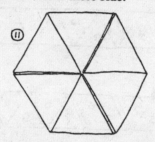

You may be wondering why you have gone through all this effort and trouble just to colour two sides of a paper hexagon. But this is where all that effort pays off, for this device has more than two sides — it has six!

This is how you find the other four.

Press any two triangles together. Then press the crease between the two opposite triangles inwards, as shown in illustrations 12 and 13.

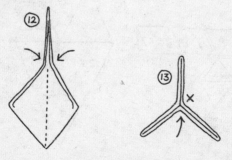

You will now discover that the central point (marked X) can be opened out. When you have done this you will find that the surface that was on top is now on the bottom, the bottom surface has disappeared inside the Hexahexaflexagon, and there is a new surface on top! Colour the new top surface and then continue turning the device inside out in the same way until you find the three remaining surfaces.

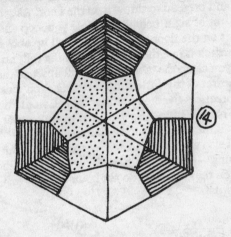

There may be occasions when the Hexahexaflexagon will not open. If this happens just try again at a different point.

If you colour the triangles in three sections as shown in illustrations 10 – 14 there are fifteen possible patterns that can be formed with the Hexahexaflexagon. About nine of these can be found fairly easily but the remaining six are very elusive.

Roll Up, Roll Up

This is an effective way of surprising a teacher during dinner. Halfway through the meal you pick up a bread roll and apparently bounce it on the floor a couple of times before proceeding to eat it.

You do not really bounce the bread roll of course. Pick up the roll and pretend to throw it on the floor. As soon as your hand is out of sight behind the table you stop and then tap your foot on the floor. Now toss the roll up above the table top and catch it in either hand. (Catch the roll, not the table top – if you catch the table top you will upset all the meals!)

The secret of this little stunt is timing. You must tap your foot at precisely the moment that the roll would have hit the floor. The roll must also be thrown back up at the right moment if the illusion is to be successful.

It will also work with an apple or an orange. But one word of warning – do not do it with school dumplings. When thrown on the floor they do not bounce – they just break the floorboards!

It Must Be Stale

Here is another little stunt you can try with a bread roll at the dining table.

Take a bread roll and tap it on the table. At the same time rap the knuckles of your other hand on the underside of the table. The taps should be timed to match the tapping of the roll. Say something like, "Wow, this one is fresher than usual," and then proceed to eat it.

You can do this little stunt on its own or combine it with the previous stunt. Take the roll and say, "This is a bit stale." Now pretend to bounce it on the floor a couple of times. Then you knock it on the table and say, "That has softened it up a bit."

These are good tricks to do when the school cook is watching. She is likely to think them so funny that she will probably join in the fun by pouring a bowl of pea soup over your head!

Lazy Letter Opener

If you and your friends are incredibly lazy, and most whizz-kids are, send your letters to one another like this.

First fold your letter in the normal way and then fold down one corner. Snip a small corner from the envelope. Place your letter in the envelope so that the point of the folded corner sticks out through the hole you have cut in the envelope. Seal the envelope in the normal way.

When your friend receives the letter he doesn't have to open it. All he has to do is hold the right end of the envelope in his right hand and the projecting corner of the letter in his left. A good sharp tug and the letter can be pulled out of the envelope. The folded edge of the letter acts as a paperknife and cuts open the envelope automatically.

Lever It

This nifty little item serves no useful purpose but it is quite intriguing.

Lay out some matches as shown. Make sure that match A is close enough to match B to ensure that the head of match C rests on the table. Now press down on the match at the bottom and the head of match C will lift from the table.

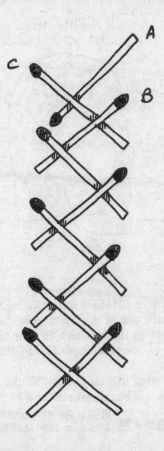

Calculating Magic

If you have a calculator or home computer you can try this amazing calculation. If you do not own such modern aids to Whizzkiddery you can try doing it in your head – there should be plenty of r _om.

Try doing it in your head

ROOM TO LET

Put the number 12345679 into your calculator. Now ask someone to pick one of the digits from that number (note there is not an 8 in the number). In your head multiply the chosen digit by 9. Now multiply 12345679 by the result you have obtained.

No matter what digit is chosen, all the numbers in the answer you get will be the same as the digit that was chosen.

Let's look at an example (yes, let's). Suppose the chosen digit was 4. 4 x 9 = 36. Multiply 12345679 by 36 and you get 444444444!

Eye, Eye!

If you want to have a quiet snooze during a lesson you could try the following technique.

Draw two eyes on a piece of paper or card and then cut them out. Close your eyes, lick the back of each paper eye and then stick them to your eyelids. Do not use super glue for this or you will never get them off.

You can now go to sleep and yet your eyes are apparently wide open!

General Knowledge Crossword

Most of the clues in this crossword are fairly straight forward to test your general knowledge. There are some, however, that will require some additional thought (sorry about that!). Watch out for clues with the words "short" or "initially" in them – it could mean that the answer is an abbreviation. If the clue was "Referee in short", for example, then the answer would be "ref". So put your thinking cap on and keep your eyes peeled (painful!).

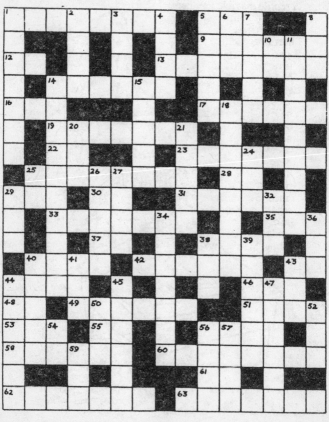

Across

1. Alfred Lord _____, famous poet (8)
5. The lot (3)
9. A meeting to contact the dead (6)
12. For example in abbreviation (2)
13. German shepherd dog (8)
14. Pioneer fliers, these brothers weren't wrong (6)
16. The cup that cheers (3)
17. Dennis is one in a well-known comic (6)
19. The first artificial satellite, launched by Russia in 1957 (7)
22. Third person singular, male (2)
23. Garment worn over clothes to keep them clean (7)
25. A reptile that lived millions of years ago (8)
28. Short company (2)
29. A moral crime (3)
30. Short reference (2)
31. A person who paints (6)
33. Yuri, the first man in space (7)
35. The Common Market in short (3)
37. In front of Bert (2)
38. A closed hand (4)
40. The Earth's only natural satellite (4)
42. The second largest continent (6)
43. Ancient city on the River Euphrates (2)
44. Man's thinking faculty (4)
46. Abbreviated manuscripts (3)
48. Third person singular of "to be" (2)
49. Arid area consisting mainly of sand (6)
51. Someone from Eastern Europe (4)
53. Large area of salt water (3)
55. Tourist Trophy initially (2)
56. Woodwind instrument (4)
58. European country south of the English Channel (6)
60. An adversary (8)
61. The indefinite article before a vowel (2)
62. The three-pronged spear of Neptune (7)
63. A basic chemical substance that cannot be split by normal means (7)

Down

1. A building for entertainment (7)
2. Not far (4)
3. What you may sing (4)
4. Tidy (4)

I know several cross words

5. A state of India (5)
6. A meadow or pasture (3)
7. Language spoken by the Romans (5)
8. Big _____, a well-known London landmark (3)
10. Not out – backwards (2)
11. To count, add up, take away, divide, or multiply (9)
14. American capital (10)
15. An oriental shrub from which a pigment is obtained (5)
18. A shocking type of eel (8)
20. Ink-filled writing instrument (3)
21. The Mohammedan Holy Scriptures (5)
24. French for King (3)
25. Diana in short (2)
26. Church instrument (5)
27. A mammal, or maybe a piece of wax on a letter (4)
29. Female equivalent of 22 Across (3)
32. A group of games in tennis (3)
34. A raging fire (7)
36. Worthless dog of low breeding (3)
38. It helps a fish balance and swim (3)
39. Strong man of the Bible (6)
40. A man who is mean with money (5)
41. Strange, it is not even (3)
43. America in letters (3)
44. A bad fit (6)
45. Towards the back of a ship (6)
47. One of two on a coat, shirt, or blouse (6)
50. Abbreviated et cetera (3)
52. A large vessel or tank for liquids (3)
54. Automobile Association initially (2)
56. Precious mineral (4)
57. What your skeleton is made of (4)
59. If you are in the Land of _____, you are asleep (3)

Answers on p128

Teacher! Teacher!

Teacher! Teacher! I keep thinking I'm a dustbin.
Don't talk rubbish.

Teacher! Teacher! My brother thinks he's a chicken.
Well, why don't you take him to a doctor?
We can't do without the eggs.

Teacher! Teacher! I keep thinking I'm invisible.
Who said that?

Teacher! Teacher! I've just swallowed my mouth organ.
Think yourself lucky that you don't play the piano.

Teacher! Teacher! I've swallowed the film from my camera.
Don't worry. Just wait and see what develops.

Teacher! Teacher! I feel like a spoon.
Well, just sit down and don't stir.

Teacher! Teacher! Everyone at school is rude to me.
Get out of here, you stupid idiot.

Teacher! Teacher! Everyone thinks I'm a liar.
I don't believe you.

Teacher! Teacher! I keep seeing spots before my eyes.
Have you seen a doctor?
No, just spots.

Teacher! Teacher! I've just lost my memory.
How did that happen?
How did what happen?

Teacher! Teacher! I've swallowed my pen.
Well, use a pencil.

Blow Your Top

The volcano on the opposite page contains the names of the twenty-three famous volcanoes listed below. They may be written horizontally, vertically, or diagonally, and they could be forwards or backwards. See how many you can find. If you do not find them all, do not get into a temper or you may blow your top.

ACONCAGUA	KILAUEA
ANTISANA	MAUNA LOA
ASAMA	MIKENO
CHILLAN	NYAMURAGIRA
DEMAVEND	POPOCATAPETL
ELBRUZ	RUAPEHU
EREBUS	SOUFRIERE
ETNA	TARAWERA
FUJIYAMA	TONGARIRO
HALEAKALA	VESUVIUS
HECLA	VILLARICA
	VOLCANELLO

you may
blow your top

Answers on p128

How To Impress Everyone

This is a great stunt if you are one of those Whizzkids who likes to show off. When you want to prove how clever you are, take a coin from your pocket and roll it across the back of your knuckles. Although it is not really difficult to master the movements needed to achieve this spectacular feat, it does require quite a bit of practice to do it fast and smoothly.

First balance the coin on the ball of your thumb, as in the first illustration. Now bring the thumb up to the forefinger until the coin can be transferred to the knuckle of that finger (illustration 2). Now move the thumb away. It is important that you position the coin so that most of it is nearest the second finger. If you don't do this the stunt will not work.

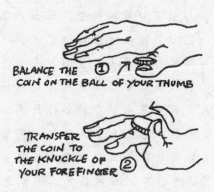

BALANCE THE ① 〳 COIN ON THE BALL OF YOUR THUMB

TRANSFER THE COIN TO THE KNUCKLE OF YOUR FOREFINGER ②

Now lower the first finger (with the coin balanced on it) and raise the second finger (illustration 3). If you now bring the two fingers together you will find that the second finger can be placed against the edge of the coin in such a way that the coin is flipped over on to the second finger.

LOWER YOUR FOREFINGER AND RAISE YOUR SECOND FINGER ③

Similar movements of the second and third fingers will transfer the coin on to the knuckle of the third finger.

The next movement is slightly different from the previous ones. This time, instead of flipping the coin on to the little finger, grip harder than before and use the little finger to pull the coin down into your hand (illustration 4). It is now a simple matter to move the coin on to the ball of the thumb. You are now ready to repeat the actions.

USE YOUR LITTLE FINGER ④ TO PULL THE COIN DOWN INTO YOUR HAND.

Don't worry if you can't do this immediately. It does take quite a lot of practice. Gradually you will find yourself doing it faster and faster until you reach the stage when it appears that the coin is rolling across the back ˙f your hand of its own accord.

You can also try doing it with both hands at the same time. That really is impressive – provided you don't knot your fingers together!

More Whizzkid Artistry

Can you see what these drawings represent?

When you have worked them out, or looked up the answers, try drawing them yourself. Your friends will be stunned at your artistic genius!

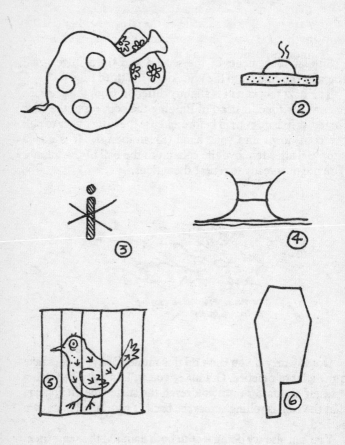

Answers on p128

Amazing Maths

Write the following sum and total on a sheet of paper:

$$462 + 307 + 299 + 101 + 134 = 1,303.$$

Show this sum to your friends and challenge them to change the sum to only three numbers which add up to 1,303. Now that sounds quite simple but there is just one stipulation – they are not allowed to write on the paper, neither can they rub anything out, and they must not cut or tear the paper.

Sounds impossible doesn't it?

But of course, it is not impossible and you show everyone how to do it. All you do is fold the paper as shown in the second illustration so that the second number (307) goes halfway across the fourth number (101) to change it to 707. Only three numbers can now be seen on the paper: 462, 707, and 134 – which add up to 1,303.

More to Amaze Your Biology Teacher

Here are some more amazing facts about the human body with which you can impress your biology teacher.

Shivering is the body's way of warming itself up in cold conditions, as when muscles shiver they generate heat in the blood. Some muscles, such as those of the fingers and the feet, have little blood in them so they are more susceptible to cold.

The scientific name for the common cold is "acute narsopharyingitis".

When you have a cold you are likely to sneeze, but did you know that it is impossible to sneeze with your eyes open? And when you do sneeze you will expel air at up to a 100 miles per hour. So don't sneeze on a motorway – you might be had up for exceeding the speed limit.

It takes about one minute for the blood to make a complete circuit through the body. In doing so it flows through some 60,000 miles of veins, arteries and blood vessels.

A man holds the record for having the longest hair. He was Swami Pandarasannadhi of India, who grew his hair until it was 7.93 metres long. The record length for a woman is a great deal less – only 2.6 metres.

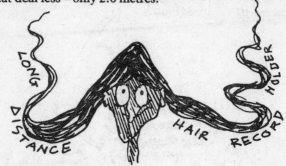

An adult man contains enough water to fill a 45 litre drum, sufficient carbon for 9,000 lead pencils, enough phosphorus to make 2,000 matches, enough fat to make seven bars of soap, enough salt to fill seven salt cellars, and enough iron to make a 5 centimetre nail.

Your ears are the only part of the body that continue to grow throughout the length of your life.

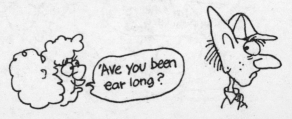

Dry Paint

Have you ever noticed that when people see a notice saying "Wet Paint" they never obey the instruction?

Just for a change, put the notice "Dry Paint" on a wall in the school corridor and watch for a while. You will find that a number of people, teachers included, will actually touch the wall to make sure that it really is dry!

You will be amazed at the reaction such a simple notice can cause – especially if the reaction of one of the teachers is to give you detention for carrying out such a dastardly deed!

Cow in the Classroom

Take a square sheet of paper and roll it diagonally around a pencil (1). Use a small piece of adhesive tape to hold the paper in place when you have finished rolling it up.

Tip out the pencil and then use a pair of scissors to make two cuts in one end of the tube so you form a triangular-shaped flap (2). Fold this flap over the open end of the tube.

If you now suck through the tube, the flap acts like a reed and produces a noise. At first this will probably sound like a frog croaking, but with practice you will be able to keep the noise going for a while so it sounds like a cow mooing.

It is not recommended that you make this noise in a classroom. Your teacher might ask you for a pint of milk!

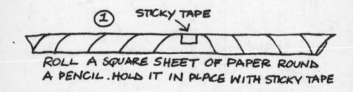

ROLL A SQUARE SHEET OF PAPER ROUND A PENCIL. HOLD IT IN PLACE WITH STICKY TAPE

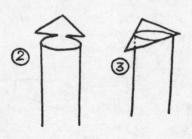

String It Up

If you ever have to carry a large or bulky item you can try this idea to make your job a little easier. It is particularly useful for paintings, boards, or other flat and reasonably slim objects. All you need is a loop of string.

The loop must be large enough to fit over both of the bottom corners of the object you have to carry. There should also be sufficient slack to enable you to reach the string when the object is held under your arm.

Put the loop around the corners, tuck the object under your arm, grab the centre of the string, and off you go! If you find that the string cuts into your hand bind a handkerchief around the centre of the string to make a padded handle.

Knock, Knock

Knock, knock.
Who's there?
Little ol' lady.
Little ol' lady who?
I didn't know you could yodel!

Knock, knock.
Who's there?
Carmen.
Carmen who?
Carmen out to play?

Knock, knock.
Who's there?
Gestapo.
Gestapo who?
Ve ask ze questions!

Knock, knock.
Who's there?
Nobel.
Nobel who?
Nobel, that's why I knocked.

Knock, knock.
Who's there?
Luke.
Luke who?
Luke through the keyhole and you'll see.

Knock, knock.
Who's there?
Alison
Alison who?
Alison Wonderland.

Knock, knock.
Who's there?
Sarah?
Sarah who?
Sarah doctor in the house?

Knock, knock.
Who's there?
Arfur
Arfur who?
Arfur got.

Knock, knock.
Who's there?
Romeo.
Romeo who?
Romeo ver the river.

Knock, knock.
Who's there?
Scot.
Scot who?
Scot nothing to do with you.

Dear Diary

Have you ever thought of keeping a diary? It can be great fun and it will only take a few minutes of your time each day. If you don't have a proper diary you can use an exercise book, or scraps of paper – it's what you put in your diary that's important, not how it looks.

A lot of people's diaries are very boring. Almost every day they write the same thing: "Got up late. Had boiled eggs for breakfast. Went to school. Came home. Did my homework and went to bed." Not very interesting is it? And when, in ten or more years' time, you come across your diary in the bottom of your drawer, it is hardly likely to remind you of what you did in a particular year!

One good way to write a diary is to simply describe the most interesting thing that happens to you each day. One day you may write about a particularly beautiful sunset you see. The next day it could be a school outing. Every day you should be able to find something that is interesting, exciting, and even sad, to put in your diary.

If you have a hobby or special interest you could devote your diary to that. Perhaps you collect stamps? Then why not record all your new stamps, any new issues, and special happenings in the stamp world? You can keep the same sort of record for any hobby: car numbers you have collected, football matches you have seen, journeys you have been on. No matter what your hobby you can find a place of it in your diary.

If you keep your diary properly it will be special to you and filled to the brim with thoughts, ideas, records and memories. It will remind you of your past when you are so famous that you need to write your memoirs! Here are diary entries from a typical week in the life of a Whizzkid.

Sunday

Mum made me go to church this morning. As I walked past the village pond a man drove his car into it. I think he was trying to dip the headlights. In church the vicar said that we're made out of dust and unto dust we shall return. When I got home I looked under my bed where there was so much dust it must have been someone coming or going.

When I went back downstairs, Mum was doing some cooking. She let me lick the cake mixture off the beaters of the food mixer. I do wish she'd turn the mixer off when she does that.

While I was in the kitchen a tramp knocked at the door and asked for food. "Didn't I give you some of my cakes a week ago?" Mum asked. "Yes," said the tramp, "but I'm better now."

Monday

A loud noise woke me early this morning. I'm not sure what it was. Perhaps it was the crack of dawn. As a result of getting up early I saw the sun rise. I think there must be lots of suns because one comes up *every* morning.

At breakfast I read in the paper that Old Masters fetch high prices at auctions. Our French teacher is pretty ancient – I wonder what sort of price he would fetch.

OLD French Master

We had exams today. I don't think I did very well. The only thing I passed was a pencil to Hortense. She is my latest girlfriend. She's not very pretty but then she's not ugly. She's a mixture of the two – pretty ugly.

After school I took the bus home – but Dad made me take it back.

Tuesday

Went to the barber today to have my hair cut. I looked at his price list and saw that he charged 90p for a haircut and 70p for a shave – so I asked him to shave my head.

He asked me how I would like my hair cut, so I said, "off". I think he must have been a policeman before he became a barber – he nicked me several times.

This evening I threw my watch out of the window. I wanted to see how time flies. When I went to bed I took a pencil with me – in case I wanted to draw the curtains.

Wednesday / Wednesday

We were given the day off school (hooray!) so Hortense and I went to the circus. The best act was the knifethrower but he was not very good. He threw lots of knives at a girl and didn't hit her once.

On the way home I asked Hortense if I could hold her hand. She said, "No thanks, it's not heavy."

I'm beginning to think my mum is an idiot. When I told her I'd brought Hortense home for lunch she said, "That's nice, dear. Put her in the freezer and we'll have her next Wednesday."

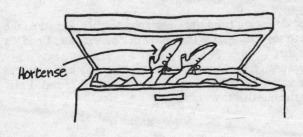

Hortense

Thursday

Had a funny dream last night. I dreamed I was awake, but when I woke up I found I was asleep.

Today was the school sports. I ran for fifteen minutes but only moved two feet – that's all I have.

Got detention from the Geography teacher. He asked the class to say what makes the Tower of Pisa lean, and I said, "a strict diet".

Because of the detention I got a later bus home. It was more crowded than my usual bus. It was so crowded that even the bus driver was standing.

Friday

At breakfast this morning Mum said she was worried about my brother Algernon biting his nails. I promised her I would cure him of that. This afternoon I kept my promise – I knocked all his teeth out.

As I walked through the market place at lunch time I was offered a pocket calculator. I didn't buy it because I know how many pockets I've got. Just past the market I saw a man fall off a ninety-foot ladder. Luckily he wasn't hurt – he only fell from the bottom rung.

Outside the supermarket an old lady told me off for pulling faces at a bulldog. It wasn't my fault – he started it.

Saturday

Today is my sister's birthday and I suppose I will have to get her a present. Last year I gave her the measles. She was lucky. All *I* got was a year older.

As a special treat Dad offered to take us all to the zoo, but I didn't want to go. If the zoo wants me they can come and get me.

When he offered me some extra pocket money I changed my mind and went, but it was a bit of a swizz. I saw a sign that said "To the Monkeys", so I followed it and saw the monkeys (one of them looked like our headmaster). Then I saw a sign that said "To the Lions", so I followed it and saw the lions. But when I followed a sign that said "To the Exit", I found myself out in the street!

It took Dad a long time to find me and I don't think he was very pleased about it. He was hoping they had put me in a cage.

SPOT THE SPACE INVADER: Number 5 is identical.

10 − 1 = 1: Take one match from the 10(×) and place it on the minus sign to change it to a multiplication sign. The sum is now 1 × 1 = 1.

LOVE LETTER: Hold the message upside down in front of a mirror and it reads "Kiss Me Dear".

IN THE DINING ROOM: In the bottom drawing: "forbidden" is underlined; marks under chin of boy drinking; drip on nose of girl (yuk!); extra line on sleeve of boy with hand in the air; spoon on table has black handle; spider has two extra legs; peas on centre plate; teacher has more spots on his cheek; right-hand boy has a nostril; eyelid of girl on the right.

BE A WHIZZKID AT ART: 1. Sign on the dotted line; 2. A spider doing a handstand; 3. A book jacket; 4. Four elephants sniffing a bun; 5. A pound note; 6. An explosion in a spaghetti factory.

ODD MAN OUT – NATURALLY: 1. Peacock – all the others are flightless birds; 2. Honey-pot – this is a type of ant, all the others are bears; 3. Armadillo – which lives in Central and South America. The others are found in Africa; 4. Pheasant – it is the only one that isn't a bird of prey; 5. Mouse – its young are born alive. All the rest develop from eggs; 6. Cypress – it is an evergreen, whereas all the others shed their leaves in winter; 7. Adder – this is a snake but the others are breeds of cats; 8. Cuscus – an Australian tree-living creature. The rest are wild members of the cat family; 9. Marmot – sometimes called "the prairie dog". It is a small burrowing rodent that lives in North America. All the rest are types of snake.

ARITHMETIC EXAM: 1. Take 2 letters (E and L) from eleven and you are left with (EL)even; 2. The answer is nothing. If you look at the last number (0) first the answer is obvious without elaborate calculation; 3. 10p and 5p. One of the coins is not a 5p piece, the other one is! 4. 19¾; 5.

6. 35. 7. 9, of course! 8. The decimal point to make the number 2.3.

ENGLISH MULTIPLE CHOICE: 1. c; 2. a; 3. b; 4. c; 5. c; 6. b; 7. a; 8. b; 9. c; 10. a; 11. c; 12. b.

LESSON MIX–UP: 1. Geography; 2. History; 3. English; 4. Mathematics; 5. Chemistry; 6. Social Studies; 7. Art; 8. Biology; 9. Algebra; 10. Latin.

GENERAL KNOWLEDGE CROSSWORD: *Across:* 1. Tennyson; 5. All; 9. Seance; 12. E.G.; 13. Alsatian; 14. Wright; 16. Tea; 17. Menace; 19. Sputnik; 22. He; 23. Overall; 25. Dinosaur; 28. Co; 29. Sin; 30. Re; 31. Artist; 33. Gagarin; 35. EEC; 37. Al; 38. Fist; 40. Moon; 42. Africa; 43. Ur; 44. Mind; 46. mss; 48. Is; 49. Desert; 51. Slav; 53. Sea; 55. T.T.; 56. Oboe; 58. France; 60. Opponent; 61. An; 62. Trident; 63. Element. *Down:* 1. Theatre; 2. Near; 3. Song; 4. Neat; 5. Assam; 6. Lea; 7. Latin; 8. Ben; 10. Ni; 11. Calculate; 14. Washington; 15. Henna; 18. Electric; 20. Pen; 21. Koran; 24. Roi; 25. Di; 26. Organ; 27. Seal; 29. She; 32. Set; 34. Inferno; 36. Cur; 38. Fin; 39. Samson; 40. Miser; 41. Odd; 43. USA; 44. Misfit; 45. Astern; 47. Sleeve; 50. Etc; 52. Vat; 54. AA; 56. Opal; 57. Bone; 59. Nod.

BLOW YOUR TOP:

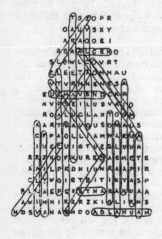

MORE WHIZZKID ARTISTRY: 1. Elephant sunbathing; 2. Egg on toast; 3. Cross-eyed; 4. Two ladies sitting on a park bench; 5. A jail bird; 6. Coffin for a one-legged man.

128